Maples
in the Mist

唐诗

何明方 译

© 1996 Times Books International
© 2006 Marshall Cavendish International (Asia) Private Limited

Published by Marshall Cavendish Editions
An imprint of Marshall Cavendish International
1 New Industrial Road, Singapore 536196

First edition by Lothrop, Lee & Shepard Books
This simplified Chinese edition published in 2006 by Marshall Cavendish International (Asia) Private Limited

Other Marshall Cavendish Offices:
Marshall Cavendish Ltd. 119 Wardour Street, London W1F 0UW, UK • Marshall Cavendish Corporation. 99 White Plains Road, Tarrytown NY 10591-9001, USA • Marshall Cavendish International (Thailand) Co Ltd. 253 Asoke, 12th Flr, Sukhumvit 21 Road, Klongtoey Nua, Wattana, Bangkok 10110, Thailand • Marshall Cavendish (Malaysia) Sdn Bhd, Times Subang, Lot 46, Subang Hi-Tech Industrial Park, Batu Tiga, 40000 Shah Alam, Selangor Darul Ehsan, Malaysia

Marshall Cavendish is a trademark of Times Publishing Limited

National Library Board Singapore Cataloguing in Publication Data

Maples in the mist : children's poems from the Tang Dynasty / translated by Minfong Ho ;
    illustrated by Jean & Mou-sien Tseng. – Singapore : Marshall Cavendish Editions, 2006.
        p. cm.
        Previously published in 1996.
        ISBN-13 : 978-981-261-345-5
        ISBN-10 : 981-261-345-5

1. Chinese poetry – Tang dynasty, 618-907 – Translations into English – Juvenile literature. I. Ho, Minfong. II. Tseng, Jean. III. Tseng, Mou-Sien.

PL2658.E3
895.11308 – dc22   SLS2006026665

Printed in China by Everbest Printing

CHILDREN'S POEMS FROM THE TANG DYNASTY

Maples in the Mist

Translated by Minfong Ho
Illustrated by Jean & Mou-sien Tseng

唐诗

张悦珍
曾谋贤 图

mc Marshall Cavendish Editions

唐诗

自序

A Note from the Translator

The Tang Dynasty (618-907 AD) is often referred to as the Golden Age of China, when the country was generally at peace and the people prosperous. During this time, the arts flourished and poetry reached new heights of sophistication. In fact, Tang poems are widely accepted as the best classical poems in China's two-thousand-year literary history. There are more than fifty thousand Tang poems by more than two thousand poets known to us, but by far the best known are the *Three Hundred Tang Poems* selected by a scholar in the eighteenth century. The poems I've translated for this book are taken from this anthology and represent the repertoire of simpler poems traditionally taught to children.

Chinese children have always learned to read by reading poetry. As adults they would be called upon to compose their own poems when they took the civil service examinations or to commemorate important events. Poetry, then, has always been tightly interwoven into the texture of Chinese life.

My own mother made me memorize many of these Tang poems when I was a child—often to her frustration and against my will. I grew up reciting these poems, even before I could read or write, and their simple images have remained vivid in my mind through the years. To me they were tantalizing little windows to a China I had never seen, and they stirred in me a curiosity about and a pride in Chinese culture.

But I never integrated the poems into my everyday life until I tried to teach them to my own children. We were living in rural upstate New York at the time, where our lives seemed nicely interwoven with Tang images—autumn maples and harvest moons, wild geese and snowy mountainsides, solitude and homesickness. In a way, I felt as if I were almost living inside these poems.

My children, however, were more interested in Big Bird on television than in the wild geese of the Tang poems. After forcing my daughter to memorize one short poem, I gave up, feeling as if I had somehow failed my mother. After all, these poems are important to me not only for their beauty, but because they form a part of that strong chain of which I am a link. My mother had recited these poems when she was a child, as had her parents and grandparents before her for more than a thousand years. I did not want to be the weak link in that chain.

And so, in an effort to bridge the linguistic gap between my mother's language and my children's, I began to translate some of the poems from Chinese to English. I don't know of any other English translations done specifically for children. Most were done several decades ago (Arthur Waley's and Amy Lowell's are perhaps the most well known) and as a result sound dated. More recent translations done by the Chinese often sound even more stilted because the translators felt compelled to retain the original rhyme schemes. In contrast, I have opted for a straight, almost literal translation.

In their originals, the poems are short and simple (every Chinese character is monosyllabic anyway, but the choices of words themselves are simple ones) and the syntax is classically symmetrical. I've tried to retain the simple vocabulary and, when possible, the parallel syntax, but I've chosen to forego the rhyme schemes and, where they come up, the literary allusions. In most cases, there is no overt subject in Chinese (the "I" is unstated and understood), so, like other translators, I have inserted personal pronouns when appropriate.

In the process of working on this book, my renewed interest in Tang poems has kindled my children's, and they have memorized a few of these poems in Chinese. Is it too much to hope that another generation of children will come to learn and love these poems, and eventually teach them to their own children as well, in one long unbroken chain?

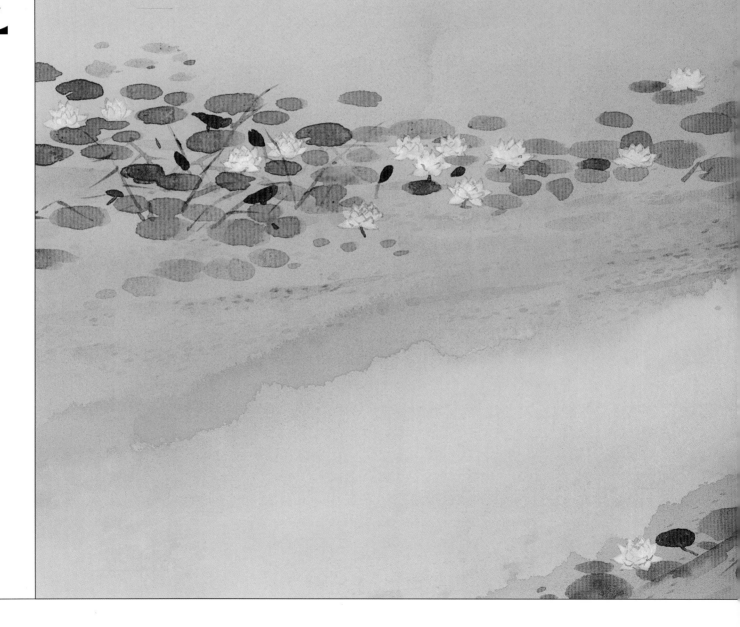

On the Pond

Little rascals paddle a little boat
Picking white lilies to steal home.
Don't you know how to hide your trail?
Your boat opens up a path in the duckweed!

— *Bai Ju-Yi*

唐诗

【池上　白居易】

小娃撑小艇　偷采白莲回　不解藏踪迹　浮萍一道开

唐诗

【小松　王建】 小松初数尺　未有直生枝　闲即傍边立　看多长却迟

Little Pine

My little pine tree is just a few feet tall.
It doesn't even have a trunk yet.
I keep measuring myself against it
But the more I watch it, the slower it grows.

— Wang Jian

【古朗月行 李白】

小时不识月 呼作白玉盘 又疑瑶台镜 飞在碧云端

Moon

When I was little
I thought the moon was a white jade plate.
Or maybe a mirror in Heaven
Flying through the blue clouds.

— Li Bai

唐诗

【枫桥　张继】

Maple Bridge

The moon drops, a crow cries, frost fills the air.
By a fishing lamp beneath the river maples I try to sleep.
Then from Cold Hill Temple outside of Ku Su Town
The sound of the midnight bell reaches my drifting boat.

— Zhang Ji

唐诗

月落乌啼霜满天　江枫渔火对愁眠　姑苏城外寒山寺　夜半钟声到客船

【咏鹅　骆宾王】

鹅鹅鹅

曲颈向天歌

白毛浮绿水

红掌拨清波

Goose

Goose! Goose! Goose!
Turn your neck and sing at the sky,
Glide your white feathers over the green water,
Paddle your red feet in the clear waves.

— Luo Bin-Wang

Meeting an Old Man

I met an old man on the road
Whose hair was as white as snow.
We walked a mile or two;
He rested four times or five.

— *Yin Luan*

唐诗

【逢老人　隐峦】

路逢一老人　两鬓白如雪　一里二里行　四回五回歇

唐诗

【游子吟　孟郊】

唐诗

慈母手中线
游子身上衣
临行密密缝
意恐迟迟归
谁言寸草心
报得三春晖

Traveler's Song

My loving mother, thread in hand,
Mended the coat I have on now,
Stitch by stitch, just before I left home,
Thinking that I might be gone a long time.
How can a blade of young grass
Ever repay the warmth of the spring sun?

— Meng Jia

唐诗

【寻隐者　贾岛】

唐诗

松下问童子 言师采药去 只在此山中 云深不知处

Looking for a Hermit

When asked, the little boy under the pine
Says simply, "My master's gone to gather herbs
Somewhere high up in these mountains,
But the clouds are so thick, I don't know where."

— Jia Dao

唐诗

【春晓　孟浩然】

春眠不觉晓　处处闻啼鸟　夜来风雨声　花落知多少

Spring Sleep

Sleepily waking to a spring dawn
I hear birds singing everywhere.
After last night's wind and rain
How many blossoms have fallen?

— Meng Hao-Ran

Riverside Song

Alone by the river the wild grass grows.
High up in the deep woods the yellow orioles sing.
The spring stream churns with the twilight storm.
Deserted, a single ferry tosses near the crossing.

— *Wei Ying-Wu*

唐诗

【滁州西涧 韦应物】

独怜幽草涧边生　上有黄鹂深树鸣　春潮带雨晚来急　野渡无人舟自横

Symmetry

A pair of golden orioles sings in the green willows,
A line of white egrets flies across the blue sky.
Through my west window, snows of a thousand autumns cap the mountains,
Beyond my east door, boats from ten thousand miles away dot the river.

— *Du Fu*

唐诗

两个黄鹂鸣翠柳 一行白鹭上青天 窗含西岭千秋雪 门泊东吴万里船

唐诗【山行 杜牧】

Mountain Road

Far up the cold mountains is a steep stone path.
Nestled in the white clouds is a little house.
We stop our cart to sit among the twilight maples;
After the frost, their leaves glow redder than spring blossoms.

— *Du Mu*

远上寒山石径斜　白云深处有人家　停车坐爱枫林晚　霜叶红于二月花

唐诗

【静夜思 李白】

床前明月光
疑是地上霜
举头望明月
低头思故乡

Quiet Night

A moonbeam by my bed
Or frost on the ground?
I look up at the full moon,
I look down and think of home.

— *Li Bai*

News of Home

You've just come from my old hometown.
You must have some news of home.
The day you left, was the plum tree
By my window in bloom yet?

— Wang Wei

唐诗

【乡事 王维】

君自故乡来 应知故乡事 来日绮窗前 寒梅着花未

唐诗

【清明　杜牧】

唐诗

清明时节雨纷纷 路上行人欲断魂 借问酒家何处有 牧童遥指杏花村

Ching Ming Day

It's raining lightly on Ching Ming Day.
On the road the travelers feel forlorn.
We ask if there's a tavern nearby.
The little cowherd points to Almond Blossom Town.

— Du Mu

唐诗

【登鹳雀楼　王之涣】

Climbing Stork Tower

The white sun sinks behind the hills,
The Yellow River rushes to the sea.
Want to see a thousand miles further?
Let's climb a little higher!

— Wang Zhi-Huan

唐诗

白日依山尽　黄河入海流　欲穷千里目　更上一层楼

唐诗

诗人小传

About the Poets

Bai Ju-Yi (772-846) *On the Pond*

One of China's most popular poets, Bai Ju-Yi was famous in his own lifetime. His almost three thousand poems were copied on the walls of inns and monasteries and sung by the dancing girls everywhere in China. His fame even reached Korea and Japan, where to this day he is honored at a festival every summer.

Born into an educated family in Hunan province, Bai Ju-Yi was recognized as a child prodigy. After passing the imperial examinations at twenty-nine, he served in a series of posts, some of them in far-flung parts of China because his criticism of official policies had offended some people in the court.

Bai Ju-Yi's life spanned the reigns of eight Tang emperors, at a time when China was caught in great political instability. He was keenly observant of and sympathetic to the suffering of the people and in later life developed a deep interest in Buddhism.

Du Fu (712-770) *Symmetry*

Du Fu's position as one of China's master poets has gone unchallenged for almost ten centuries, yet he often thought of his own life as a series of frustrations and failures. Born into a family of literary distinction, he grew up with a strong sense of Confucian duty to his emperor and country. Despite this background, however, Du Fu failed the imperial examinations three times. He was finally given a minor position in the Crown Prince's palace when he was forty-three.

At forty-seven, he left the imperial service and settled in Chengdu, where he spent his most peaceful and productive years. Half of his still existing 1,450 poems were written during this period.

During the last five years of his life, Du Fu took a long river journey down the Yangtze. The river might have taken him home to Hunan, but midway he became ill and spent two years at Kwei-Chou, a famous site overlooking two gorges. There he wrote his last poem while lying sick on a riverboat and died shortly after.

Du Mu (803-852) *Mountain Road, Ching Ming Day*

The eldest of a literary family in Shensi, Du Mu was a distinguished essayist and poet. He passed the imperial examinations when he was twenty-five and was duly posted to official appointments in various provinces. There, in famous old cities such as Lo-Yang and Yang-Chou, Du Mu cultivated a reputation for appreciating striking scenery and beautiful women, both of which he wrote about with great delicacy.

Ching Ming Day is an annual spring festival during which families gather to sweep and clean their ancestors' gravesites.

Jia Dao (779-843) *Looking for a Hermit*

One of the later Tang poets, Jia Dao was from Northern China, near what is now Beijing. Many of his poems allude to the mystical interplay between man and nature, and influenced the "Ching Hu" style of poetry during the following Sung Dynasty.

Li Bai (701-762) *Moon, Quiet Night*

Generally considered China's single best poet, Li Bai's poems are praised for their flow and energy (known in Chinese literary criticism as *chi* or breath). He spent his boyhood in Szechuan province, but when he was twenty-four, he left home to explore the world of central and eastern China. He only gained imperial recognition decades later, when he was given a position at the famous Hanlin Academy, but he fell out of favor due to court intrigues three years later and returned to the hills. His restlessness and Taoist nonchalance about fame and wealth have become legendary.

Luo Bin-Wang (640-684?) *Goose*

Talented even as a young boy, Luo Bin-Wang wrote this poem when he was only seven years old. He became a restless adventurer and for years wandered all over China. When he was eventually appointed a petty officer, he got involved in an attempt to assassinate Empress Wu Zetian. When this failed, he disappeared —some say he was killed, others that he became a monk.

Meng Hao-Ran (689-740) *Spring Sleep*

A native of Hupeh, Meng Hao-Ran was about ten years older than Wang Wei and Li Bai, both of whom admired his poetry. When he failed the civil service examination at forty, he took off on a long journey in the mountains of the central Yangtze region and lived as a recluse. Most of his more than two hundred poems were written during this period.

Meng Jia (751-814) *Traveler's Song*

Although his poetry was celebrated in his lifetime, Meng Jia's long life was filled with many failures and he was often poor and bitter. His wife and three sons all died young, and he failed the imperial examinations several times before finally passing in his forties. He was then assigned to a minor post, which he lost because of incompetence. He spent the rest of his life living off friends and patrons. Still, he transcended his personal suffering in his poems.

Wang Jian (766-830) *Little Pine*

Born into a poor family, Wang Jian was a soldier, courtier, official, and recluse during various phases of his long life. His collection of a hundred "Palace Poems" is particularly well known and is said to be based on actual incidents that happened in Emperor Te-tsung's harem.

Wang Wei (701-761) *News from Home*

Renowned as both a poet and painter, it is often said of Wang Wei that "in his poetry there is painting; in his painting there is poetry." His life was not unlike many of the Tang poets. Considered a prodigy in his teens, he was awarded a government post which later led to various promotions and then banishments to remote outposts of the Chinese empire. Unlike many other Tang poets, however, Wang Wei deliberately chose to withdraw from active society for long periods. Even while holding office in the capital, he led the life of a recluse in a mountain hut, where he spent many quiet years studying Buddhist scriptures. His poems reflect both his love of landscape painting and his devout Buddhism.

Wang Zhi-Huan (688-742) *Climbing Stork Tower*

Little is known about Wang Zhi-Huan, but from his epitaph it is evident that he was considered a great poet during his day. Except for six poems, all his work has been lost to us. Those six, however, are rated as exquisite gems of Tang poetry.

Wei Ying-Wu (737-792) *Riverside Song*

A native of the capital city of Ch'ang-An, Wei Ying-Wu served as an imperial guardsman and later in various provincial posts. Wei's poetry reflects the gentle serenity characteristic of the "Idyllic Nature" school.

Yin Luan (dates unknown) *Meeting an Old Man*

Although his simple poem has delighted generations of Chinese children, very little is known of Yin Luan himself.

Zhang Ji (766-830?) *Maple Bridge*

Not much is known of Zhang Ji. He is thought to have come from a humble family and to have become a civil servant in 799. The actual Maple Bridge in Suchow has been made so famous by this poem that it has, through the centuries, become a place of pilgrimage for poetry lovers.